2laa

The Old Mission Cook

Recipes for Using and Preserving Our Local Produce

Michelle E. Keith
Anam Cara Farm
Old Mission, MI

Published by Anam Cara Farm
PO Box 157, Old Mission, MI 49673
keith@mileader.com

Additional copies of this book are available through major online bookstores or participating local retail outlets.

Proceeds from the sale of this book are donated to local programs supporting the education of migrant worker children.

ISBN-13: 978-1475074918
ISBN-10: 1475074913

The Old Mission Cook

Recipes for Using and Preserving Our Local Produce

Table of Contents

Dedication

This cookbook is dedicated to my mother, my grandmothers, my high school home ec teacher, and all the other women who have shared their know-how and recipes with me over the years. They have taught me more than Martha Stewart ever will.

Thanks, also, to Ruth Virkus (arguably the best cook in our family) for reviewing and editing this book.

Introduction

First, a disclaimer. I don't pretend to be a great cook. I enjoy cooking, and I especially enjoy cooking for family and friends. I enjoy reading recipe books and magazines, clipping new recipes to try. And I did grow up in farm country (Iowa), participated in 4-H, and took six years of home ec classes in school. But I am a long way from being a "master chef." Plain and simple is the way I like to cook.

I also don't pretend to be a great gardener. I enjoy having a big garden each year. And I enjoy eating fresh veggies and fruits straight from our own garden or grown locally on Old Mission Peninsula. But you'll find only the basics in our garden—we're pretty much corn, beans, and tomatoes people.

So why did I put a cookbook together? There are three main reasons. First, I needed to get myself organized. I've collected so many cook books and clipped so many recipes that when it comes time to prepare something, I can't remember where the recipe is. When I'm faced with a big bucket of ripe tomatoes, for example, I need to figure out several ways to creatively use or preserve it all. My recipes and canning instructions are currently spread out over several books and files.

Second, I figured that as long as I was getting organized, I might as well type it all up in one place and share it with others. Someday, the grandkids may be interested in growing and preserving their own food, too. It might also be useful to any other "kids" who grew up someplace other than farm country and are interested in eating more natural, local foods.

Third, now that it is so easy to self-publish, I thought, *Why not put it together, sell it to others interested in eating locally, and donate the money to a good cause?* Old Mission (including our farm) depends so much on the help of migrant workers. Therefore, the profits from this book will be donated to local programs that support the education of migrant workers' children. This is one small way to show our appreciation.

What's in this recipe book? You'll notice that the book is arranged by type of produce, rather than the typical categories of Salads, Main Dishes, Desserts, etc. This is because when a particular produce item is in season, we tend to eat a lot of it and need to do something with it—quickly. So if you have a lot of one item, you'll find several different ways to use it.

You'll also notice that, for the most part, the recipes are simple and don't have a lot of exotic ingredients. While I like to cook, I don't like to spend a lot of time in the kitchen agonizing over complicated recipes. People won't take a bite of my food and remark, "Oh, is that a hint of fennel?" Generally, if I can't buy an ingredient at the Mapleton Market or at a local farm stand, you probably won't see it in these recipes. For example, you won't see a section on oranges or mangoes, or see a recipe using fresh ginger.

I do like to "cook with wine." (More usually goes in me than in the recipes.) So you'll also notice that each produce item includes what I call a "Preparation Libation"—a recommendation of a local Peninsula wine that will taste good when working with that particular fruit or vegetable. Take advantage of our great local wines—I do!

In addition to the recipes, each produce item also has recommendations regarding picking, storing and preserving.

There is nothing better than eating fresh and local. **So, enjoy the best of Old Mission!**

I read recipes the same way I read science fiction. I get to the end and I think, "Well, that's not going to happen."
HistoricLOLS.com

Canned Goods

(Excerpts from a song by Greg Brown)

Let those December winds bellow 'n' blow
I'm as warm as a July tomato.

Peaches on the shelf
Potatoes in the bin
Supper's ready, everybody come on in
Taste a little of the summer,
You can taste a little of the summer
my grandma's put it all in jars.

Well, there's a root cellar, fruit cellar down below
Watch your head now, and down you go
Maybe you're weary an' you don't give a damn
I bet you never tasted her blackberry jam.

She's got magic in her - you know what I mean
She puts the sun and rain in with her green beans.
What with the snow and the economy and ev'rything,
I think I'll jus' stay down here and eat until spring.

When I go to see my grandma I gain a lot of weight
With her dear hands she gives me plate after plate.
She cans the pickles, sweet & dill
She cans the songs of the whippoorwill
And the morning dew and the evening moon
'N' I really got to go see her pretty soon
'Cause these canned goods I buy at the store
Ain't got the summer in them anymore.

You bet, grandma, as sure as you're born
I'll take some more potatoes and a thunderstorm.

Peaches on the shelf
Potatoes in the bin
Supper's ready, everybody come on in, now
Taste a little of the summer,
Taste a little of the summer,
My grandma put it all in jars.

APPLES

Nothing says fall like crisp, fresh apples. Plus it's a fruit that you can eat local all winter long.

Preparation Libation:

A natural choice would be ***Kroupa Orchards Apple Wine, from Peninsula Cellars***

Picking and Storing Fresh Apples

Pick before daytime temperatures are below freezing. Blemish-free apples store best. Put in a cool, dark place, away from other produce. Apples should remain edible through the winter.

Applesauce

This is a good way to preserve a lot of apples, especially ones that have a few bruises or bad spots. If you leave the skins on, the sauce takes on a pinkish color.

Cut up, remove blemishes, and core enough apples to fill a large cooking pot (about 25). Using a variety of kinds is best—Ida Reds, MacIntosh, Honeycrips, Delicious, etc.

Add:
1-1/2 c. water
1/2 c. lemon juice
1 c. honey
Ground cinnamon, nutmeg, and cloves to taste (I use 1 t. cinnamon, 1/2 t. nutmeg, and 1/4 t. cloves.)

Simmer 20 minutes or until apples are tender. Drain if needed. Press through sieve; freeze in quart-size plastic containers. Makes about 12 cups.

Easy Apple Butter

A nice treat on toast, muffins, or pancakes.

12 c. apples—peeled, cored and sliced
2 c. sugar
1/3 c. water
2 T. cider vinegar
2 t. cinnamon
1/4 t. ground cloves
1/8 t. allspice
1/8 t. nutmeg

Place apples in a 3-4 quart slow cooker. Stir in remainder of ingredients. Cover and cook on high heat 5-6 hours. Cool, then ladle into freezer containers, leaving 1/2" head space.

Makes 4 cups.

Apple Salad with Apple Cider Vinaigrette

This is a great seasonal salad to serve company.

Vinaigrette Dressing:
1 c. apple cider (or apple juice)
1/4 t. black pepper
1/8 c. apple cider vinegar
1/4 t. salt
1/4 t. cinnamon
1/8 c. honey
1/2 c. vegetable oil

Mix and refrigerate up to 5 days.

(continued on next page)

Salad:
Arrange on plates:
Mixed baby greens
Julienned green or tart apples (dip in lemon juice or Fruit Fresh to keep from turning brown)
Spiced walnuts
Crumbled blue cheese
Chopped cucumber

Add diced cooked chicken breast to make it a lunch or dinner main course. Serve with vinaigrette dressing.

Waldorf Salad

A classic fall salad from the 1950's.

1/2 c. mayonnaise
1/2 c. sour cream
1 c. celery, chopped
1/2 c. coarsely chopped walnuts
1 T. honey
1-1/2 c. tart apples—peeled, cored and diced
1 c. seedless grapes, halved

Combine mayo, sour cream, honey. Add apples and mix well. Add rest of ingredients, mix, and chill.

Apple Crisp

A yummy dessert, as good as pie.

Filling:
6 apples, peeled, cored, and thinly sliced
Zest of 1 lemon
Juice from 1/2 of a lemon
2 T. sugar
1 T. flour

(continued on next page)

Topping:
1-1/4 c. flour
6 T. brown sugar
2 T. sugar
1/4 t. salt
1/2 T. cinnamon
1 t. ground ginger
1/2 t. ground cloves
2/3 c. pecans ground in food processor until almost as fine as flour
2/3 c. roughly chopped pecans
12 T. (1-1/2 sticks) cold butter, cut into small pieces

Preheat oven to 375°. Combine all filling ingredients in a large bowl.

To make topping: In another bowl, combine flour, sugars, salt, spices, and nuts. Add butter pieces and quickly work them into the mix using your fingertips, until they are evenly distributed and about the size of peas.

Butter the bottom and sides of a 9 x 12 baking pan and spoon in apple mixture. Spread topping over apples, patting down with your hands and making sure no fruit is uncovered. Bake 40-50 minutes, until top is golden brown. Serve while hot with vanilla ice cream on top.

Deep Dish Apple Pie

You can make your own crust recipe, but the Pillsbury rolled crusts from the refrigerator section of the grocery store taste almost as good—especially as prepared in this recipe.

7-9 apples, peeled and sliced (use your favorite apple variety, but golden delicious work well)
1 c. sugar
2 T. flour
1 t. cinnamon
Dash of nutmeg
Dash of salt
2 T. butter
Crust for a 2-crust pie
1 egg white, mixed with 1 t. water

Combine sugar, flour, spices, salt. Mix with apples.
Place 1 crust in 9" deep dish pie pan; fill with apple mixture—it will be heaping. Dot butter on top of the apples. Put on top crust and crimp edges together. Brush top with the egg white; sprinkle with a little sugar. Cut 3 slits in top crust. Place on a baking sheet (to catch the drips) and bake at 400° for 50 minutes or until bubbly and browned.

It isn't so much what's on the table that matters, as what's on the chairs.

-W. S. Gilbert

ASPARAGUS

One of the first vegetables of spring—it goes great with early barbeques. While best eaten fresh, it can be frozen as well.

Preparation Libation:

Give the cook a crisp, cool glass of ***Chateau Grand Traverse Dry Riesling.***

Picking and Storing Asparagus

Cut asparagus spears when they are 6-10" tall, before they've flowered out. Use a knife to cut just below soil level. Store them upright in the refrigerator, with the cut ends in a container of water. Use within a few days.

Freezing Asparagus

This is the easiest way to preserve extra asparagus. When thawed, the stalks won't be as firm as when fresh, but will be usable cut up in baked recipes.

Use young green stalks. Rinse, trim. Sort by size. Blanch in boiling water—thicker stalks for 4 minutes, thinner spears for 2 minutes. Run under cold water. Put in quart-size freezer bags. You could also cut them into 1" lengths before blanching—they'll be easier to put in recipes when thawed.

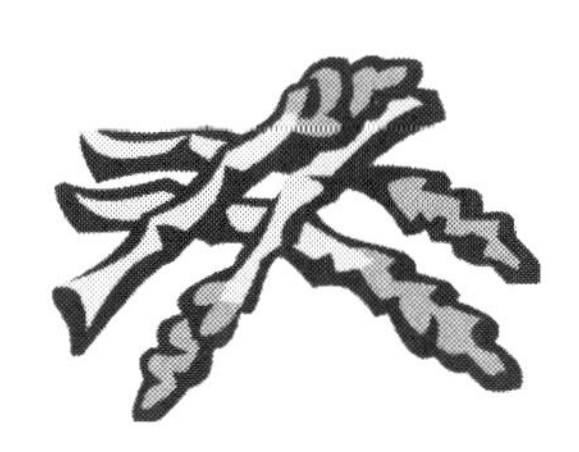

Steamed Asparagus

The plain and simple way to enjoy the fresh flavor.

Clean, trim fresh asparagus spears. I like to peel off all the pointy tips on the stalks. Place in microwave-safe dish with 1/2" of water and 2 t. lemon juice. Cover loosely with wax paper or plastic wrap. Microwave on high for 2 minutes or until crisp tender.

Grilled Asparagus

Another easy way to prepare—especially if someone else is "manning" the barbeque!

Rinse fresh spears and dry on paper towel. Trim woody ends and peel. Place in baking dish and coat with olive oil, sprinkle with salt and pepper. Transfer to a grill pan and grill over medium heat until softened but not limp—about 8 minutes.

Grilled Vegetables

I wait all winter to enjoy this favorite on the grill! Use a bottled sweet or Vidalia onion salad dressing—I like the Tastefully Simple brand best.

Mix together:
1/4 c. olive oil
1/2 t. garlic powder
2 T. honey
1/8 t. pepper
1 t. dried oregano
2T. bottled onion salad dressing

(continued)

Toss in:
1 lb. fresh asparagus (about 1 bunch), trimmed and cut into bite-size pieces
6-7 baby carrots, cut lengthwise
Sweet red pepper strips (about half of a large pepper)
1 medium red onion, cut into wedges and separated

Marinate up to 1-1/2 hours in refrigerator.
Place veggies in grilling pan. Grill 8-12 minutes, stirring occasionally, until crisp-tender.

Roasted Asparagus with Parmesan

The roasting brings out the best flavor of asparagus.

1 lb. fresh asparagus (about 1 bunch)
3 T. olive oil
1/2 t. salt (sea salt is best)
1/2 t. pepper
2T. lemon juice
Grated parmesan cheese

Heat oven to 450°. Trim and peel woody tips off the asparagus, cutting off tough ends. Drizzle half the olive oil on a baking sheet. Spread asparagus in a single layer on the sheet. Drizzle with remaining olive oil and toss to coat. Sprinkle on salt and pepper. Roast for 8 minutes. To serve, place in serving dish, sprinkle lemon juice over the asparagus and sprinkle with grated cheese.

As a child my family's menu consisted of two choices: take it, or leave it.

-Buddy Hackett

Asparagus Breakfast Casserole

A good breakfast for company.

2 c. fresh or frozen asparagus, cut in 1-inch pieces
1 c. cubed cooked ham
1 small sweet red pepper, chopped
2 c. shredded cheddar cheese
1 small onion, chopped
8 eggs, beaten
3 T. butter
2 c. low-fat milk
8 c. cubed day old French-type bread
1/3 c. honey
1/2 t. salt
1/2 t. pepper

In skillet, sauté the asparagus, red pepper and onion in the butter until tender. Set aside.

Place bread in greased 12 x 9 baking dish. Layer with ham, 1 cup of the cheese and vegetable mixture. Sprinkle with remaining cheese. In large bowl, combine the eggs, milk, honey, salt and pepper. Pour over the top. Cover and refrigerate overnight.

Remove from refrigerator 30 minutes before baking. Bake uncovered at 350° for 40-45 minutes or until a knife inserted near the center comes out clean. Let stand 10 minutes before cutting.

Asparagus Mushroom Quiche

A good make-ahead breakfast that can be warmed up piece-by-piece (whenever everybody wakes up).

1 refrigerated pie crust
1 lb. fresh or frozen asparagus, cut into 1" pieces
1 medium onion, chopped
1 c. sliced fresh mushrooms
2 T. butter
3 eggs
1-1/3 c. heavy whipping cream
2 t. minced fresh basil
1/2 t. salt
1/2 t. pepper

Unroll pie crust into a 9" pie plate; flute edges. Steam the asparagus in a covered microwave-safe pan with about a half-inch of water, until crisp-tender—about 3-5 minutes.

Sauté onion and mushrooms in butter in skillet until tender. Stir in asparagus. Transfer to crust. Whisk the eggs, cream, basil, salt and pepper in a small bowl; pour over top. Bake at 375° for 30-35 minutes or until a knife inserted near the center comes out clean. Let stand for 10 minutes before cutting. Can refrigerate and reheat pieces in the microwave, for about a minute each.

The act of putting into your mouth what the earth has grown is perhaps your most direct interaction with the earth.

-Frances Moore Lappe

Asparagus Fritters

These taste almost like the great asparagus tempura on the Boathouse Restaurant's menu.

1 c. cold water
2/3 c. yellow cornmeal
1/2 c. flour
1/3 c. cornstarch
1 egg, lightly beaten
1 t. baking powder
Vegetable oil for deep-fat frying
1 lb. thick asparagus, woody ends trimmed
1/2 c. Dijon-style mustard
2 T. snipped fresh dill weed
2 T. honey

For batter, in large bowl whisk together water, cornmeal, flour, cornstarch, egg, baking powder, and 1/2 t. salt until combined. Batter will be lumpy.

In large skillet, heat about 1" of oil to 350°. Working with 3 or 4 spears at a time, dip asparagus into batter, letting excess batter drip back into dish. Slide spears into hot oil and fry 3-4 minutes, until golden. Remove with tongs; drain on paper towels. After draining, keep warm by placing on a baking sheet and storing in a 200° oven. Meanwhile, in a small bowl combine the mustard, dill week, and honey for the dip.

BEETS

A tasty mid-summer source of potassium, vitamin C and iron.
I like them plain, so you won't find pickled beets here!

Preparation Libation:

*The **Bowers Harbor Vineyard Cabernet Franc** should be sturdy enough to drink while working with beets.*

Picking and Storing Beets

Harvest when the beets are 1-1/2 to 2" in diameter. I haven't had much luck with keeping beets in a root cellar, so I usually cook or roast them, then slice and freeze.

Cooking Beets

This is just like boiling whole potatoes. Boil red beets and golden beets separately or the colors will run.

Cut ends off. Boil until beets are soft enough to stick a fork in the center. Drain and cool. Peel. Slice. Eat warm or cold.

Freezing Beets

Cook as above. Freeze slices in containers or freezer bags. Thaw and use warm or cold.

Roasted Beets

Scrub beets, cut off ends. Place in a baking dish and add enough water to cover bottom of pan. Cover with foil. Roast in a 350° oven for 1 hour. Let cool. Remove skins.

Beet Salad

At Wolfgang Puck's Spago restaurants, they spread the goat cheese on thin beet slices, making 4 layers; then quarter the slices. It looks beautiful, but this "less arranged" salad tastes just as good.

Arrange baby mixed greens on salad plates.
Top with sliced beets, crumbled goat cheese, and chopped pecans or walnuts. Serve with raspberry vinaigrette (We think Ken's Steakhouse brand is best.)

Layered Beet and Raspberry Salad

A very fancy way to present a salad for a group.

Raspberry Vinaigrette:
1 c. raspberries
3 T. sugar
3 T. red wine vinegar
4 T. balsamic vinegar
1/2 t. salt
Black pepper
1 c. extra-virgin olive oil

Salad:
1 container mixed greens
6 golden or red beets, roasted/cooked, peeled and sliced
4 oz. crumbled goat cheese
1 pint fresh raspberries

To prepare vinaigrette, combine berries and sugar in a saucepan. Cook over medium heat until berries release juices and sugar dissolves. Remove from heat and press through a strainer to remove seeds.

Place berry mixture in food processor. Add vinegars, salt and pepper, and pulse. Drizzle in olive oil while processing, until thickened.

(continued on next page)

To prepare salad, place layer of greens in bottom of clear glass bowl. Place sliced beets in a circle on top. Sprinkle with goat cheese, then with raspberries. Drizzle with about 1/4 of the vinaigrette, and repeat layers. Serve with leftover vinaigrette.

Russian Borscht

You either like beet soup, or you don't. Here's a recipe for those who do!

1/2 c. finely chopped carrots
1 c. finely chopped onions
2 c. peeled, finely chopped uncooked beets
1 T. butter
2 c. beef stock
1 c. finely shredded cabbage
1 T. apple-cider vinegar
5 T. sour cream
Heaping 1/4 c. grated cucumber

Place carrots, onions and beets in large soup pot. Add enough boiling water to barely cover; simmer, covered, for about 20 minutes. Add butter, stock, cabbage and vinegar; simmer 15 minutes more. You could process with an immersion blender, if you don't like it chunky.

Combine sour cream and grated cucumber. Place soup in serving bowls; top each bowl with dollop of sour cream-cucumber mixture. Makes 4-5 servings.

Chocolate Beet Cake

If you crave beets, doesn't this sound really good?!

Cake:
3/4 c. unsweetened cocoa powder, plus extra for pans
3 large red beets, cooked, skinned and quartered
2 sticks unsalted butter, softened
2-1/4 c. sugar
4 large eggs, room temperature
1 t. vanilla
2-1/2 c. flour
2 t. baking soda
Pinch of salt

Icing:
8 oz. cream cheese, softened
1 stick unsalted butter, softened
1 t. vanilla
1 c. powdered sugar

Preheat oven to 350°. Butter two 9" layer pans, line with parchment paper; butter the paper. Sift extra cocoa powder into pans and tap out the excess. Puree beets in food processor. Measure 2 c. and set aside. With electric mixer, cream butter and sugar until fluffy. Beat in eggs, one at a time. Add the beet puree and vanilla; mix well. In large bowl, mix together cocoa, flour, baking soda and salt. Add to wet ingredients; mix on low speed until smooth and combined. Divide batter evenly between pans and bake for 40-45 minutes, rotating halfway through, until toothpick inserted in the center comes out clean. Cool in pan for 10 minutes, then turn out and cool on a rack.

To make the icing, beat cream cheese with electric mixer until smooth. Beat in butter until smooth. Beat in vanilla. Add confectioner's sugar by hand. Then beat with electric mixer until smooth. Use right away. Place one cake layer on a pan and frost top with half the icing. Top with second layer and frost with remaining frosting. Leave sides unfrosted.

BLUEBERRIES

When it's July and blueberry season is on, go to Buchan's Blueberry Hill and stock up for the whole year!

Preparation Libation:

You should have fun when working with this easy fruit, so pick ***Chateau Chantal's Virtue*** *to accompany you.*

Picking and Storing Blueberries

Pick when fully blue and ripe. They can be stored for several days in the refrigerator in a ventilated container. Blueberries are the best and easiest fruit to put away in the freezer and use all winter long. They are almost as good frozen and thawed as they are fresh.

Freezing Blueberries

Rinse and drain. Place in quart freezer bags. When thawed, they can often be used in place of fresh berries.

Blueberry Smoothie

A healthy and easy breakfast. You can substitute yogurt for the Kefir, which is a yogurt-like beverage found in the dairy section.

1 c. frozen blueberries
1 c. vanilla-flavored Kefir
1 T. agave nectar or honey

Place all ingredients in blender and blend until smooth. If you like it sweeter, put in one packet of Truvia. Makes one large smoothie.

Blueberry Pie

Forget apple, peach or cherry pie. If you want to score points for making a homemade pie, blueberry is the absolute easiest and is almost foolproof!

1/2 c. sugar
1/3 c. flour
1/2 t. cinnamon
4 c. blueberries (fresh, or frozen and thawed to room temp)
1 T. lemon juice
Crust for 2-crust pie (Pillsbury rolled crusts are good)

Stir together sugar, flour, and cinnamon. Mix with the berries. Place one crust in bottom of regular (not deep dish) pie plate and fill with berries. Sprinkle with lemon juice. Put on top crust, crimp, and put 3 slits in the top. Sprinkle with sugar. Bake at 425° for 35-45 minutes. (If you want to make a deep dish pie, all measurements would be heaping.)

Very Berry Pie

A good no-bake way to serve fruit.

1-3/4 c. Cool Whip, divided
1 graham cracker pie crust
1 c. fresh raspberries
1 c. fresh blueberries
1 T. sugar or equivalent Splenda
1 c. cold milk
1 package (1 oz.) instant white chocolate pudding mix

Spread 1/4 c. whipped topping in the crust. Combine berries and sugar. Spoon 1 cup of the mixture over the whipped topping. In a bowl, whisk the milk and pudding mix for 2 minutes; let stand for 2 minutes or until soft-set. Spoon over berries. Spread with remaining whipped topping, then with remaining berries. Refrigerate for 45 minutes or until set.

Blueberry Cobbler

6 c. fresh or frozen blueberries
1-1/2 c. sugar
1/4 c. water

Crust:
3/4 c. butter, softened
1-1/2 c. plus 2 T. sugar, divided
3 eggs
1 t. vanilla extract
1-1/2 c. flour
1 t. baking powder
1/2 t. salt
1/4 c. butter, melted

Place blueberries in greased 13 x 9 baking pan.
In small saucepan, bring sugar and water to a boil; cook and stir until sugar is dissolved. Pour over berries.

In small bowl, cream butter and 1-1/2 c. sugar until light and fluffy. Add eggs, one at a time, beating well after each. Stir in vanilla. Combine the flour, baking powder and salt; add to creamed mixture. Spread over berry mixture. Drizzle with melted butter; sprinkle with remaining sugar.

Bake at 350° for 40-45 minutes or until golden brown. Serve warm with ice cream.

Blueberry Bread Pudding

3 eggs
4 c. heavy whipping cream
2 c. sugar
3 t. vanilla
2 c. fresh or frozen blueberries
1 pkg. (10-12 oz.) white baking chips
1 loaf (1 lb.) French bread, cut into 1 inch cubes

Sauce:
1 pkg. white baking chips
1 c. heavy whipping cream

In large bowl, combine the eggs, cream, sugar and vanilla. Stir in blueberries and baking chips. Stir in bread cubes. Let stand 15 minutes or until bread is softened.

Put in greased 13 x 9 baking dish. Bake, uncovered, at 350° for 50-60 minutes or until a knife inserted near the center comes out clean. Let stand for 5 minutes before serving.

For sauce, place baking chips in a small bowl. In a small saucepan, bring 1 c. cream to a simmer. Pour over chips. Stir until melted. Serve over pudding.

Blueberries and Cream Pops

A fun and healthy treat for the kids.

1-1/2 c. fresh or frozen blueberries
1/4 c. sugar
1-1/2 c. vanilla yogurt, divided

In a blender, puree blueberries with sugar and 1/2 c. vanilla yogurt until smooth. Spoon about half the mixture into popsicle molds, equally among the molds. Spoon 1 c. vanilla yogurt equally among the molds, over the blueberry layer. Spoon in remaining blueberry mixture. Freeze.

Blueberry Bottom Pie

2 pkg. (4-serving size) JELLO vanilla flavor pudding and pie filling
1-1/4 c. milk
1-1/2 c. blueberries, pureed in blender
1/2 t. cinnamon
1 pre-baked 9-inch pie shell (regular or shortbread flavor)
2 t. grated lemon rind (or equivalent Real Lemon)
3-1/2 c. thawed Cool Whip

Combine 1 package pie filling mix, 1/4 c. of the milk, the pureed berries and cinnamon in a saucepan. Cook and stir until it comes to a full boil. Pour into pie crust; chill. Prepare remaining package pie filling mix with remaining milk as directed on package for pie. Add 1 t. of the lemon rind; pour into bowl and cover with plastic wrap. Chill about 1 hour until cold (or place in freezer for 30 minutes). Fold in 1 c. of the whipped topping and spoon over blueberry layer. Combine remaining whipped topping and lemon rind. Spoon over filling. Freeze 1 hour or chill in refrigerator 3 hours before serving. Garnish with blueberries and mint leaves, if desired.

Eat, drink, and be merry, for tomorrow we may diet.

-Harry Kurnitz

CHERRIES

Traverse City's signature fruit! July brings out the pit-spitter in all of us!

Preparation Libation:

You might as well go full-on Cherry, and enjoy ***Chateau Grand Traverse Winery's National Cherry Festival Wine*** *while cooking with this fruit. CGT's* ***Cherry Riesling*** *is also a good option.*

Picking and Storing Cherries

There are a few U-Pick cherry stands on Old Mission Peninsula, if you don't have your own trees. You may be able to get fresh tart cherries that way. Sweet cherries, being firmer, will keep for several days in the refrigerator and are what you will find at the roadside stands. Tart cherries need to be processed right away. Personally, I would rather buy canned, frozen, or dried tart cherries than pit them all myself. Every cook in the Traverse City area, however, needs to be able to serve something with a cherry flair, so here are some ideas that aren't too labor-intensive.

Center Road Cherries

This is the all-time favorite way to enjoy cherries.

1. Stop at a fruit stand and buy 1 quart of dark sweet cherries.
2. Eat, spitting pits out the car window, being careful to avoid the bicyclists.
3. When finished, stop at another fruit stand. Repeat.

Cherry Bounce

As far as I'm concerned, this is the best way to preserve tart cherries. It makes a fun red holiday drink that can really sneak up on you if you aren't careful! (Right, Mom? ☺)

Fill a gallon-size crock with fresh tart cherries, unpitted. Add 1 c. sugar. Cover with (cheap) vodka. It will take about a fifth of vodka for a gallon crock. Cover and put on a shelf until Christmas. Drain the liquid and toss out the cherries. Mix with 7-up to serve.

Crock Pot Oatmeal

A healthy and easy breakfast that's put together the night before.

2 c. milk (or 1 c. milk and 1 c. half-and-half
1 c. old fashioned or steel-cut oats
1/4 c. real maple syrup
1 c. peeled and chopped apples
1 T. butter
1/4 c. brown sugar
12 t. cinnamon
1/2 c. dried cherries
1/2 c. walnuts, pecans, or almonds

Spray crock pot with cooking spray. Add all ingredients, stir and cook on low 8-9 hours. Stir and serve. Makes 4 small portions.

Baked Oatmeal

Another healthy make-ahead breakfast.

4 c. old fashioned oatmeal
3 t. baking powder
3 t. cinnamon
3/4 t. salt
1 c. brown sugar
4 eggs, lightly beaten
1-1/2 t. vanilla
1 c. milk
1 c. unsweetened applesauce
3/4 c. dried cherries
1/2 c. pecan pieces

Preheat oven to 325°. Spray 2-1/2 qt. baking dish with cooking spray. Mix oatmeal, baking powder, cinnamon, salt, and brown sugar. In another bowl, mix eggs, vanilla, milk, and applesauce. Add to dry ingredients. Stir in cherries and nuts. Bake 40-45 minutes until light golden brown. Cool in pan, then cut into 8 or 10 servings. Store in covered container in refrigerator. Pop one into microwave for 1 minute and serve with milk.

Cherry Chicken Salad

You'll find this on the menu of several local restaurants.

Arrange on salad plates:
Mixed greens or chopped romaine
Dried cherries
Red onion, thin sliced and separated
Pecans
Feta cheese, crumbled
Grilled chicken breast strips

Top with Raspberry-Pecan vinaigrette (Ken's Steakhouse brand is our favorite.)

Cherry Pie

Here is the classic pie recipe for when you have to make the real thing.

4 c. tart cherries, pitted
1-1/3 c. sugar
1/2 t. almond extract
2 T. butter
3 T. cornstarch or quick cooking tapioca
1/8 t. salt
Pastry for a 2-crust 9" pie.

Mix cherries with sugar, extract, cornstarch and salt. Pour into pie shell, dot with butter. Put top crust on. Bake at 425° for 10 minutes, and at 350° for another 30 minutes. Let cool to room temperature before serving.

Gorp Cookies

These cookies have it all—cherries, chocolate, nuts, and oatmeal.

2 c. flour
2-1/2 c. rolled oats (quick-cooking or regular)
1 t. salt (kosher preferred)
1 t. baking soda
1/2 t. ground cinnamon
2 sticks butter, softened
1 c. brown sugar, packed
1/2 c. sugar
2 eggs
2 t. vanilla
8 oz. chopped chocolate—white or semi-sweet
1 c. chopped pecans or walnuts
1 c. dried cherries

Preheat oven to 350°. Stir together flour, oats, salt, soda, cinnamon. Cream butter, eggs, and vanilla. Add to flour mixture. Stir in chocolate, nuts, and fruits. Drop on parchment lined cookie sheet by tablespoons. Bake 15-18 minutes. Dough can be refrigerated or frozen.

Cherry Almond Drop Scones

A good alternative to muffins in the morning.

Combine in a bowl:
2-1/4 c. flour
2T. sugar
2-1/4 t. baking powder
1/2 t. baking soda
1/2 t. salt

Combine, then stir into dry ingredients:
1 c. low-fat vanilla yogurt
1 egg, lightly beaten
1/4 c. butter, melted
1/4 t. almond extract

Fold in 1/2 c. dried cherries and 1/2 c. slivered almonds.

Drop by heaping tablespoonfuls 2" apart on baking sheet coated with PAM. Bake at 400° for 15-18 minutes or until lightly browned. Serve warm.

Cherries Jubilee

For those who like to live dangerously....

2 lbs. dark sweet cherries, pitted
1/4 c. sugar
1/2 c. water
2 t. cornstarch
1 T. grated orange peel
1/2 c. brandy
1 pound cake, sliced, or vanilla ice cream

Combine sugar, cornstarch, and water in a sauté pan. Cook, stirring constantly until smooth and clear (about 5 minutes.) Add cherries and orange peel. Heat thoroughly. Gently heat brandy, separately. Pour over the top of the heated cherries. Flame it in front of your company, if desired, by using a one-click lighter. Stir, then ladle over cake or ice cream.

Cherry Biscotti

A little labor intensive, but the cookies keep a long time.

3/4 c. sugar
1/2 c. chopped walnuts
2 eggs
1 t. baking powder
1/4 c. vegetable oil
1/4 t. salt
1 T. orange juice
1 c. dried tart cherries, chopped
2 t. grated orange peel
1 egg white
1-1/2 t. vanilla
1 T. water
2 c. flour

Combine sugar and eggs in large bowl. Beat with mixer at medium for 3-4 minutes until thick and pale yellow. Add oil, orange juice, orange peel and vanilla. Beat another 1-2 minutes. Combine flour, walnuts, baking powder and salt; gradually add to egg mixture. Stir in cherries by hand.

Turn dough onto lightly floured surface. Sprinkle with additional flour and knead. Shape into 2 8" x 2" logs. Place on greased baking sheet and flatten tops slightly. Combine egg white and water; brush on logs. Sprinkle with more sugar.

Bake at 350° for 25-30 minutes, until light brown and firm to the touch. Let cool on baking sheet 15 minutes.

Reduce oven temp to 300°. Cut logs diagonally into ½ inch slices with serrated knife. Arrange slices, cut side down on baking sheet. Bake 8-10 minutes; turn slices. Bake another 8-10 minutes until golden brown. Let cool completely. Makes about 30 cookies.

CORN

Being from Iowa, August means having corn on the cob for supper as the main dish (with a ripe tomato on the side.)

Preparation Libation:

A nice ***Two Lads Cabernet Franc Rose*** *would go great with the process of prepping corn.*

Picking and Storing Corn

Harvest when the silks are brown and the ears are filled out. (If you break a kernel, whitish corn "milk" will flow.) Process or eat corn as soon as possible after picking for the sweetest flavor, otherwise the sugars will start to break down. Corn purists will put the water on to boil before they go out to pick. The best way to preserve corn is to freeze it.

Freezing Corn

Husk corn and remove silks. Get water boiling in large pot. Blanch by placing a few ears in, bringing back to boil, then boiling for 1 minute. Remove from water, let cool a bit. Cut corn off ears. Place in quart freezer bags. To use, steam the frozen corn with water and butter, and maybe a little milk.

Corn on the Cob – Plain and Simple

Get a big pot of water boiling. Husk corn and remove silks. Place ears in pot and bring back to boiling. Boil about 5 minutes until the corn is a nice, golden color. Serve with lots of butter, salt and pepper.

The Proper Way to Butter Corn on the Cob

If you want to start a good argument, try to impose your way of buttering corn on someone else. Various methods include:

- Trying to use a knife and spreading the butter on the ear, all nice and proper
- Rolling the ear on a stick of butter in the butter dish
- Buying a fancy corn buttering utensil from an expensive kitchen store
- Slathering butter on a slice of bread, placing the bread in the palm of your hand, and rolling the ear in the buttered bread (obviously the best way to do it, as far as I'm concerned...)

Cheesy Corn Bites

An appetizer with a different twist.

8 oz. cream cheese, room temperature
1 c. shredded pepper jack cheese
1 egg
1/2 c. frozen corn kernels
48 scoop-shaped tortilla chips (one 10-oz. bag)
Chopped chives, for sprinkling

Preheat oven to 350°. In a large bowl, mix the cream cheese, pepper jack cheese, egg and corn. Arrange the chips on a large rimmed cookie sheet and place 1 t. corn mixture in each. Bake until the filling sets, about 20 minutes. Sprinkle with chives; serve warm.

Corn Salad

A nice seasonal salad dish.

4 T. lime juice
1 T. honey
1/2 c. chopped green or red pepper
3 T. fresh chopped cilantro (or equivalent dried)
1/4 t. salt
4-5 ears corn, cooked and cut off cob
1 c. chopped carrot
1-1/2 c. baby spinach
1 c. cut up cherry tomatoes
3/4 c. chopped cucumber

In large bowl, whisk lime juice and honey. Stir in pepper, cilantro, salt. Add corn and mix. Add remaining ingredients and mix. Serve immediately, or cover and chill for up to 1 hour. Serves 10.

Corn Chowder

An easy way to have "home-made" soup.

4 slices bacon, cooked and cut in small pieces (or Bacon Bits)
1 10-3/4 oz. can Campbell's cream of potato soup
1 c. milk
1-1/2 c. corn (fresh or frozen)

Heat soup, milk and corn in saucepan. Add cooked bacon and heat until chowder is simmering. Makes 2 servings.

Ask your child what he wants for dinner only if he's buying.

-Fran Lebowitz

Corn Casserole

A good side dish for Thanksgiving.

1 egg
1 c. sour cream
1/3 c. butter
1-1/2 to 2 cups fresh/frozen corn
1 can creamed corn
1 box Jiffy corn bread mix

Mix and put in 8 x 8 casserole dish. Bake at 350° for 45 minutes. Let sit 5 minutes before serving.

Corn Pudding

It's a side dish—not a dessert!

1 stick butter, melted
3 c. fresh corn kernels
2 eggs
1 c. sour cream
9 oz. Monterey Jack or pepper Jack cheese, cut into 1/2-inch cubes
1/2 c. cornmeal
1 4-oz. can green chiles, drained, diced
1/2 t. salt
1/2 c. grated Parmesan cheese

Preheat oven to 350°. Butter a 2-quart casserole dish. In blender or food processor, puree 1 c. corn kernels with melted butter and eggs.

In large bowl, combine all remaining ingredients except Parmesan cheese. Add pureed corn and mix well. Pour into casserole dish, sprinkle with Parmesan, and bake for 30 minutes, until puffed and golden.

CUCUMBERS

While you can get cukes in the store all winter long, they taste best right out of the garden in mid-summer.

Preparation Libation:

*Try the **Black Star Farms' Red House Red** while slicing and dicing your cukes.*

Picking and Storing Cucumbers

Pick cucumbers when they turn dark green, but don't leave them on the vine too long, or they will lose their flavor. They will store several days in the refrigerator. The only good way to preserve them for longer periods of time is to pickle them.

Refrigerator Bread and Butter Pickles

This is so easy, and the pickles stay good in the refrigerator for several months.

1 gallon cucumbers, peeled and sliced about 1/4" thick (about 8 large cukes)
4 thin-sliced white onions

Alternate layers of cukes and onions in a large container. Sprinkle 1/2 c. of salt on top (kosher or pickling salt preferred); cover with ice cubes. Let stand 2-4 hours; drain.

1/2 c. salt
4 c. vinegar
4 c. sugar
1-1/2 t. celery seed
1-1/2 T. mustard seed
1-1/2 T. turmeric

Bring remaining ingredients to a boil; cool. Pour over drained cukes and onions. Put in one large glass container, or in quart jars. Store in refrigerator. Wait 2-3 days before eating.

Dill Pickles

3 lb. small cucumbers
4 c. water
4 c. white vinegar
1/2 c. sugar
1/3 c. pickling salt
6 T. dill seeds

Slice cukes into 1/4 to 1/2 inch thick slices. In large pot combine water, vinegar, sugar, and pickling salt. Bring to boiling.

Meanwhile, prepare jars. Pack cucumbers loosely into hot, pint canning jars, leaving 1/4" headroom. Add 1 T. dill seeds to each jar. Pour hot vinegar mixture into jars, leaving a 1/2" headspace. Discard any remaining vinegar mixture. Wipe jar rims, top with lids. Process in a boiling water canner for 10 minutes. Remove and cool on racks. Let stand 1 week before eating.

Cucumber Rounds

A good "old-school" appetizer.

8 oz. cream cheese, softened
1 pkg. Good Seasons Dry Italian dressing mix
1 loaf cocktail rye bread, or similar
1 cucumber, thinly sliced
Dill weed

Mix dressing mix with cream cheese. Spread on bread slices. Place slice of cucumber on top of cheese and sprinkle on a bit of dill weed. Cover and refrigerate until serving time.

Fresh Vegetable Salad

Simple, but good

3 c. thinly sliced cucumbers
3/4 c. chopped red onion
1/2 c. each chopped green, red and yellow peppers
1/2 c. cider vinegar
2 T. sugar

In large serving bowl, combine the cucumbers, onion and peppers. In a small bowl, whisk vinegar and sugar. Pour over veggies; toss to coat. Chill until serving.

Creamy Dill Cucumbers

Another great addition to a summer picnic.

1 c. skim milk
1/2 c. low-fat mayonnaise
1/2 c. reduced fat sour cream
1 envelope ranch salad dressing mix
2 T. dill weed
1/8 t. celery seed
1/8 t. pepper
2 large cucumbers, peeled and sliced
2/3 c. sliced red onion, separated into rings

In a small bowl, combine the milk, mayo, sour cream, dressing mix, dill, celery seed and pepper. Stir in the cucumbers and onion.

Cucumbers with Dressing

An old favorite for those who like creamy cukes.

1 c. mayonnaise
1/4 c. sugar
1/4 c. vinegar
1/4 t. salt
4 c. sliced cucumbers

In a bowl, combine mayo, sugar, vinegar and salt. Add cucumbers; stir to coat. Cover and refrigerate for 2 hours.

Never eat more than you can lift.

-Miss Piggy

GRAPES

This chapter refers to your garden "table grapes"—not your good wine grapes! Table grapes will be ready to eat in late summer, earlier than when wine grapes are ready.

Preparation Libation:

A jelly glass jar full of Mogen David-style wine would probably be appropriate, because that's what my Grandpa used to make from his garden grapes. (Horrid, but very strong!) I'd rather enjoy a ***Brys Estates Pinot Noir****.*

Picking and Storing Grapes

Cut grape clusters off the vines when they are fully purple and taste sweet. They will store in the refrigerator just a few days, and must be processed soon. The best way to preserve table grapes is to make jelly (if you don't make your own strong and horrid wine at home.)

Grape Jelly

This is a little labor-intensive, but the jelly is great. Or as one grandchild said, "Better than the real stuff you get in the store!"

Remove red grapes from stems. Pulse slightly in food processor. Prepare enough to fill a large pot. Simmer 5-10 minutes. This gets the juice running and turns the juice purple.

Strain through a metal strainer. Refrigerate juice overnight to let sediment settle. Then strain again through cheesecloth. You will need to end up with 5 cups of prepared juice.

(continued on next page)

Measure 7 c. of sugar and set aside.

Put 5 c. of juice in large pot. Stir in 1 box of Sure-Jell (pectin). Add 1/2 t. butter. Bring mixture to full rolling boil on high heat, stirring constantly. Stir in sugar all at once. Return to full rolling boil and boil exactly 1 minute, stirring constantly. Remove from heat and skim off foam.

Ladle quickly into clean, sterilized jelly jars. Fill to within 1/8" of tops. Wipe rims clean, seal, and boil in hot water bath canner for 5 minutes.

GREEN BEANS

Green beans are the garden's "utility player"—easiest to grow, easiest to preserve, very prolific, and useful in many ways all year long.

Preparation Libation:

A nice ***Chateau Chantal Pinot Gris*** *will go well with the preparation of your buckets and buckets of green beans.*

Picking and Storing Green Beans

Try to pick the beans while they are still young and slender—before they get fat and tough. They will keep several days in the refrigerator, especially when in a Debbie Meyer Green Bag. Beans freeze so easily, I don't think it is worth the effort to can them.

Freezing Green Beans

Having a big stash of green beans in the freezer will help get you through the winter!

Medium size beans work best (not too thin or too fat.) Rinse and trim off ends of beans. Cut into pieces about 1-1/2" long. Get a large pot of water boiling. Blanch in boiling water, working in small batches. (To blanch, put in an amount of beans that won't bring the water temperature down too much at a time. Once the water gets back to boiling, boil just 30 seconds to a minute. Immediately take out and rinse in cold water. It helps to use a large slotted spoon or slotted ladle)

Place in 1-quart freezer bags. You can then reheat the beans by steaming them with a bit of water and butter. Or you can thaw and use in casserole recipes.

Green Beans with Peanuts

A little fancier way to serve fresh beans.

6 c. green beans – fresh or frozen
1 t. dried ginger
1 T. soy sauce
1 t. peanut oil
1 t. garlic paste (or 1 clove garlic)
3 T. chopped roasted peanuts

Steam beans until tender. Drain. Combine ginger, soy, oil, and garlic in hot skillet. Sauté beans and oil mixture 5 minutes. Sprinkle with peanuts.

Green Bean Casserole (traditional)

This is the standard Thanksgiving side dish.

2 cans (10-3/4 oz. each) Campbell's Cream of Mushroom Soup
1 c. milk
2 t. soy sauce
1/4 t. black pepper
8 c. cooked cut green beans
1 6-oz. can French's French Fried Onions

Stir soup, milk, soy sauce, pepper, beans and 1-1/3 c. fried onions in 3 qt. casserole. Bake at 350° for 25 minutes or until hot. Stir. Top with remaining onions. Bake for 5 minutes more.

Green Bean Casserole (Alternative Version)

2 c. green beans
1 can bean sprouts
1 can cream of mushroom soup
1 8 oz. can water chestnuts
1 6-oz. can French fried onion rings

Mix and bake 1/2 hour at 350°. Add onion rings on top and bake 10 minutes more.

Doggie Diet Food

If you have a dog who needs to lose weight, but is always hungry, you can substitute thawed green beans for some of their meal. (Double-check with your vet, of course, before trying this with your dog.) It fills up their tummy, but doesn't give them many calories. Our Labs love to eat green beans, and will even pluck them raw out of the garden for a snack.

God almighty first planted a garden: and, indeed, it is the purest of human pleasure.

-Francis Bacon

MAPLE SYRUP

In early March, you can usually spot the sugar shacks on Old Mission burning off the sap to make this precious commodity. It takes about 40 gallons of sap to make one gallon of syrup.

Preparation Libation:

Old School White from Peninsula Cellars *will go well with your maple syrup concoctions.*

Processing and Storing Maple Syrup

You can buy an expensive collection and evaporator system to make a large quantity of syrup, or you can collect and process a small batch with a few taps, buckets, and a big outdoor cooking pot. There are entire books on how to do this properly. My only advice is: Do not try to boil down all of the sap inside the house—you'll ruin your dry wall and wallpaper. I'd store real maple syrup in the refrigerator. It will keep for several months.

Maple Oatmeal Muffins

1 c. quick-cooking or regular rolled oats
1/2 c. milk
1 c. flour
2 t. baking powder
1/4 t. salt
1/4 t. cinnamon
3/4 c. pure maple syrup
1/4 c. butter, melted
1 egg, lightly beaten
1/2 c. chopped pecans

(continued on next page)

Line 12 muffin cups with paper baking cups; set aside. In medium bowl, combine oats and milk; let stand for 5 minutes. In large bowl, combine flour, baking powder, salt and cinnamon. Set aside.

Stir maple syrup, melted butter and egg into oats mixture. Add egg mixture all at once to flour mixture. Stir just until moistened. Fold half of the pecans into the batter.

Spoon batter into muffin cups, filling 2/3 full. Sprinkle with remaining nuts. Bake in a 400° oven 15-18 minutes, or until tops are gold and toothpick inserted in center comes out clean.

Maple Salad Dressing

This is sweet and tangy like a French dressing.

7 T. maple syrup
1/4 c. cider vinegar
1/4 c. ketchup
3 T. plus 1 t. oil (canola or vegetable)
2 T. water
1/2 t. prepared horseradish
1/4 t. salt
1/8 t. celery salt

Combine all ingredients in a jar with a tight-fitting lid; shake well. Refrigerate until serving.

Maple Syrup Cake

2-1/2 c. cake flour or 2-1/4 c. all-purpose flour
2 t. baking powder
1/2 t. baking soda
1/2 t. salt
1/2 t. ground ginger
1/2 c. butter, softened
1/2 c. sugar
1 egg, lightly beaten
1 egg yolk, lightly beaten
1 c. pure maple syrup
1/2 c. hot water
1/2 c. chopped walnuts, toasted

Grease and flour a 10" fluted tube pan. In medium bowl, mix flour, baking powder, soda, salt and ginger; set aside.

In a large bowl, beat butter with electric mixer 30 seconds. Add sugar; beat until well-combined. Add egg, egg yolk, and maple syrup; beat 1 minute more. Alternately add flour mixture and hot water to butter mixture, beating on low speed after each addition. Spoon batter into cake pan; spread evenly.

Bake in 375° oven 45 minutes or until toothpick inserted near center comes out clean. Cool for 10 minutes, then remove cake from pan. Cool completely. Spoon Maple Icing over cake; sprinkle top with walnuts.

Maple Icing:
In medium bowl, beat 1/2 c. powdered sugar and 2 T. softened butter with an electric mixer until combined. Beat in 1/4 c. pure maple syrup. Beat in 1 c. additional powdered sugar. Add 2-3 t. milk, 1 t. at a time until it is drizzling consistency. Makes 1 cup.

ONIONS

Plant a variety of onions in your garden (bunching, red, white, yellow) for goodness all season long. Onions are found in many recipes throughout this book, so these are recipes where onions are the main ingredient.

Preparation Libation:

Try ***Chateau Grand Traverse Semi-Dry Riesling*** *with your onion prep.*

Picking and Storing Onions

Bunching onions can be pulled at any time they are the right size. They are generally used fresh.

For red, yellow and white onions, pull from ground when they are the size you want, and place in a single layer on newspapers, in a dry place out of the sun for a few days until skins and tops are dry. Store in a cool, dry, dark place. They will keep for several months.

Freezing Onions

You can also preserve onions by freezing them. Peel and chop onions, then place in quart freezer bags. Freeze, and then pull out quantities as needed in recipes.

French Onion Soup

Simple ingredients that are so tasty together.

3 T. butter
4 large onions, halved and thinly sliced
2 T. flour
2 14-oz. cans beef broth
6 slices French bread, sliced about 1/2 inch thick (you could use croutons in a pinch)
1/4 pound Gruyere or mozzarella cheese (you can also use provolone slices if that's what you have on hand)

Melt butter in deep pot. Add onions, cover and cook about 15 minutes until onions are very soft and begin to turn brown. Uncover, stir in flour and cook 1 minute. Stir in broth and 1 cup water. Simmer, uncovered, 5 minutes.

Pre-heat broiler. Spread bread slices on a baking sheet. Toast under broiler about 1 minute on each side. Set aside. Place 6 ovenproof soup bowls on baking sheet. Divide soup evenly among bowls. Place slice of toasted bread on each serving. Top with thin slices of cheese. Heat under broiler for 3 minutes or until cheese is melted.

Onion Rings

2 eggs
1/2 c. milk
1 c. flour
1 t. baking powder
1 t. salt
2 t. melted shortening

Beat eggs and milk. Add other ingredients and mix well. Peel a large sweet onion. Slice cross-wise 1/4 inch thick. Separate into rings. Dip into batter, then drop into an inch or two of hot vegetable oil (400°) and fry until golden brown. Drain on paper towels.

Onion Pie

1 c. finely crushed soda crackers
1/4 c. butter, melted
2 c. thinly sliced onions
2 T. butter
3/4 c. milk
2 eggs, beaten
3/4 t. salt
Dash of pepper
1/4 c. grated cheese (Mozzarella or Monterrey Jack)

Mix crackers and melted butter; press in a 9" pie plate. Fry the onions in the butter until soft. Put in the pie shell. Mix milk, eggs, salt and pepper and pour over onions. Top with grated cheese. Bake at 350° for 30 minutes.

PEACHES

August brings peaches to the fruit stands on Old Mission. Enjoy them while you can—the season doesn't last long.

Preparation Libation:

Celebrate peach season with ***Chateau Chantal's Celebrate!*** *sparkling wine.*

Picking and Storing Peaches

Pick peaches when the fruit has become soft and juicy (not hard and crunchy), with a little red blush on the skin. If you have some that are a little under-ripe, you can place them in a brown paper bag on your kitchen counter for a couple days and they will ripen up. You will need to eat them, use them, or can them within a few short days. I haven't had good luck freezing peaches, so the best way to preserve them is to can them.

Canned Peaches

This is an easy way to enjoy the taste of fresh peaches all year long. We like to eat them for dessert just plain, right out of the jar. Or they could be drained and used in recipes.

Boil water in large pot and boil peaches a few at a time for 1 minute to loosen skins.

Skin peaches and cut into chunks, removing the pits. Pack the chunks in clean quart jars. Cover the peaches with syrup, leaving 1/4" headroom.

(continued on next page)

Syrup:
2 c. honey
2 c. water

Briefly boil together. This syrup recipe is enough to cover 7 quart jars of peaches. Run a knife around the side of the jars to get out all of the air pockets. Wipe rims, cover with lids and place in boiling hot water bath canner.

Boil in hot water bath canner for 30-40 minutes. Store in dark, cool place up to several months.

Peach Fuzz

Fiber AND alcohol! How perfect is that?!

2 fresh peaches
1 6-oz. can frozen lemonade concentrate
6 oz. vodka
Crushed ice

Slice peaches into blender. (Leave skin on.) Add lemonade, vodka, and fill with crushed ice. Blend until well mixed. Serves 4 (or 2, if you're really thirsty.)

Peach Jam

8-10 fresh peaches, peeled, and cut into chunks.
3 c. sugar
1 T. plus 1 t. lemon juice
1/2 t. coarse salt

Working in batches, pulse peaches in a food processor until chunky. Transfer to a saucepan and add sugar, lemon juice, and salt. Bring to a boil, stirring frequently. Boil, continuing to stir, until bubbles slow, foam subsides, fruit rises to the top, and jam sticks to a spoon when lifted, about 12 minutes. Let cool. Refrigerate in glass containers, for up to 2 months.

Peach Pie

We love, love, love peach pie!

Crust for 2-crust pie
10 ripe, but firm, peaches
Juice of 1 lemon, or equivalent Real Lemon
1/2 t. almond extract
2/3 c. flour
1 c. sugar
1/2 t. cinnamon
1/8 t. nutmeg
1/2 t. salt
3 T. butter
1 egg white

Peel and cut peaches into 1/4" thick slices (about 7 cups). Toss with lemon juice and almond extract. In another bowl, stir together the flour, sugar, cinnamon, nutmeg and salt. Stir flour mixture into the peaches and mix well. Put peaches into the pie crust. Scatter with pieces of butter. Place top crust on. Mix egg white with 1 t. water and brush on crust.

Bake at 450° for 10 minutes, then lower heat to 350° and bake another 50 minutes. May need to cover edge of crust with foil to keep it from getting too brown. Cool at least 30 minutes before serving.

Peach Cobbler

Another great peachy dessert.

Filling:
4-5 c. sliced peaches (fresh or canned peaches, drained)
1/4 c. brown sugar
1 T. flour

(continued on next page)

Dough:
1-1/2 c. flour
1-1/2 t. baking powder
3/4 t. salt
4 T. butter, cut into cubes
3/4 c. milk

Preheat oven to 425°. Grease a 9" deep dish pie plate. Put fruit in bowl, sprinkle with brown sugar and flour. Stir and set aside in refrigerator.

Mix the dough—flour, baking powder, salt and sugar. With pastry blender, cut in the butter until crumbly. Add just enough milk to form a moist dough. Press the dough into the pie plate. Pour fruit on top and bake for 40 minutes. Serve warm with ice cream.

Peach Crumble

The oatmeal in this is a good touch.

1 c. packed brown sugar
1 c. flour
1/2 c. steel-cut oats
1 stick of butter, cut into cubes and softened
1 t. cinnamon
1 t. nutmeg
1 pound of fresh peaches

Preheat oven to 350°. Place 9" pan in oven to warm. In large bowl, use pastry blender to combine the brown sugar, flour, oats, butter, cinnamon and nutmeg. Peel and slice peaches into 6-8 wedges each. Place wedges in bottom of the warm pan. Top with crumble mix and bake 15-20 minutes until the crumble is golden brown.

Peaches and Cream Dessert

A fancier dessert, for company.

1 16 oz. package pecan shortbread cookies, crushed
1/2 c. butter, melted
1 c. sugar
1 3 oz. package peach Jello
2 T. cornstarch
1 12-oz. can lemon-lime soda (7-Up or Sprite)
1 8 oz. package cream cheese, softened
1 c. powdered sugar
1 8 oz. carton frozen whipped topping, thawed
6 c. fresh peaches, peeled and sliced
1/3 c. unsweetened pineapple juice

In a small bowl, combine the cookie crumbs and butter; press into the bottom of an ungreased 13 x 9 inch dish.

In a small saucepan, combine the sugar, Jello, and cornstarch; stir in soda until smooth. Bring to a boil. Cook and stir for 5-7 minutes or until slightly thickened. Cool to room temperature, stirring occasionally.

Meanwhile, in large bowl, beat cream cheese and confectioners' sugar until smooth. Beat in whipped topping until blended. Spread over crust. Combine peaches and pineapple juice. Arrange over cream cheese layer. Pour gelatin mixture over top. Cover and refrigerate overnight.

Peach-Blueberry Pie

A good combination of two local fruits.

2 single pie crusts
5 c. peeled, sliced fresh peaches
1 c. fresh or frozen blueberries, thawed
1/3. c. packed brown sugar, plus 2 T.
2 T. cornstarch
1/2 t. cinnamon

Preheat oven to 375°. Line a 9-inch pie plate with one crust. Set aside.

In large bowl combine peaches, blueberries, 1/3 c. brown sugar, cornstarch, and cinnamon. Place filling in crust. Cut remaining crust into 1-inch wide strips. Weave strips over filling in lattice pattern. Press strip ends into bottom pastry. Seal and crimp. Sprinkle lattice with 2 T. brown sugar.

Cover edges with foil. Bake on baking sheet 25 minutes. Remove foil and bake 25 minutes more or until filling is thickened and crust is golden. Cool on rack.

"The most remarkable thing about my mother is that for 30 years, she served the family nothing but leftovers. The original meal has never been found."

- Calvin Trillin

PEPPERS

Sweet or hot—take your pick! Just remember to wear rubber gloves when cutting the jalapenos!

Preparation Libation:

Try a little ***Otis from Bowers Harbor Vineyard*** *while you are picking your peck of pickled peppers. (Say that 3 times fast after you've had a glass or two.)*

Picking and Storing Peppers

If you plant sweet bell peppers, you can pick them when they are green, or if you wait until they turn red, they'll be a little sweeter. Pick jalapeno peppers when they are dark green and full size. Peppers will keep in the refrigerator several days. The easiest way to store them long term is by freezing or making pepper jelly.

Freezing Peppers

Chop red, green or yellow peppers into 1/4" chunks. Place in quart freezer bags and freeze. You can then pull out as needed and use in recipes, throw in omelets, or put on a salad.

Vodka from Hell

If you like a little extra kick in your Bloody Mary, try this!

Cut 6 jalapeno peppers in half lengthwise; remove seeds, tops, and core. Cut into small pieces and place in a quart jar. Fill jar with vodka. It will be ready to drink in 2-5 days.

Pepper Jelly

This makes a great appetizer when served on top of cream cheese with crackers. Being green, it's great at Christmas or St. Patrick's Day.

2/3 c. finely chopped jalapeno peppers
2-1/2 c. apple juice
1/4 c. apple cider vinegar
1 drop green food coloring
5-1/2 c. sugar
1 box Sure-Jell

Prepare and clean 6 half-pint jars, rims and lids. Prepare peppers. Measure sugar and place in a bowl. Place peppers, apple cider vinegar and apple juice into a large pot. Stir in the Sure-Jell. Bring mixture to a full rolling boil. Stir in sugar quickly. Return to full rolling boil and boil exactly 1 minute, stirring constantly. Remove from heat. Ladle into jars, filling to within 1/8 inch of tops. Wipe jar rims and threads. Place in boiling water canner and boil 5-10 minutes. Remove and let cool. It will take about 1 week to set.

Pepper Salad

This is a simple salad that will help you fill up your plate with vegetables.

Chop into 1/4 inch pieces:
1 red pepper
1 orange pepper
1 green pepper

Place in bowl and sprinkle with 1 T. lime juice. Stir, and serve.

POTATOES

Potatoes taste so incredibly good when eaten straight out of the garden—they are worth every carb. Yukon Gold potatoes grow really well in the Old Mission climate and offer a better taste in recipes than russets from the store.

Preparation Libation:

Two Lads' Pinot Grigio *will make the potato peeling a lot more fun!*

Picking and Storing Potatoes

Dig up potatoes when they are the size you want. It's easiest to dig up a whole plant with a pitchfork, but you can also just hand dig and pull off a few potatoes from each vine, then recover the roots. Brush dirt off.

If you want to store them, spread out in a single layer on newspaper, and put in a dry place out of direct sunlight. Let "harden" for 2-3 days until skin is dried. Turn over if necessary. Place in bins, then keep in dark, cool place. They will keep several months. If they start to sprout, you could cut them up next spring and use them for seed potatoes.

Warning: Do not let your dog eat raw potatoes, especially green or rotting ones. They can get really sick. So be sure not to leave any stray potatoes in your garden.

Broasted Potatoes

This is an easy way to prepare potatoes for a crowd.

Quarter potatoes lengthwise, with skins on.
Brush with melted butter. Sprinkle with parmesan cheese and your favorite spices (salt, pepper, basil, chives). Bake on cookie sheet in 375° oven for an hour, turning over once.

Colcannon (Irish Potatoes)

A St. Patrick's Day favorite.

2-1/2 pounds potatoes, peeled and cubed
4 slices bacon
1/2 small head cabbage, chopped or shredded
1 onion, chopped
1/2 c. milk or half-and-half
1/4 c. butter, melted
Salt and pepper

Put potatoes in saucepan with enough water to cover. Bring to a boil and cook until tender, about 15-20 minutes.

Cook bacon in skillet. Remove bacon, crumble and set aside. In bacon drippings, sauté cabbage and onion until soft and translucent, about 10 minutes.

Drain potatoes; mash with milk. Add salt, pepper, bacon, cabbage, and onions. Transfer to serving bowl. Make a well and pour in butter.

Oven-Roasted Red Potatoes

Another easy way to serve spuds.

2 pounds red potatoes, sliced into 1/2 inch thick rounds
1/3 c. vegetable oil
1 envelope dry onion soup mix

Combine all ingredients in a large plastic bag; shake until well coated. Empty onto an ungreased 13 x 9 baking pan. Cover and bake at 350° for 35 minutes, stirring occasionally. Uncover and bake 15 minutes longer or until potatoes are tender.

Hemmingway's Shrimp Chowder

Thanks to the chef at Hemmingway's restaurant in Orlando for sharing his recipe.

1/2 lb. bacon, cut into chunks
1 c. onion, diced
1/4 c. diced red pepper
3 potatoes, cooked and diced
1/4 c. flour
1 8-oz. jar clam juice
2 c. water
Salt, pepper
1 c. half-and-half, heated
1 c. cooked corn
1 dozen cooked shrimp, cut into pieces

Fry bacon in large pot. Add onion and cook until tender. Add pepper and potatoes. Add flour and cook 3-4 minutes. Whisk in clam juice and water. Bring to a simmer. Add hot half-and-half and simmer until slightly thickened. Season with salt and pepper. Add shrimp and corn. Simmer, then serve.

Basic Potato Soup

Just basic ingredients here, but it is my favorite comfort food.

6-8 medium potatoes
1 onion, chopped
6 T. butter, divided
3 T. flour, more if needed
1-1/2 c. milk

Melt 3 T. butter and saute onions until tender. Peel and cut potatoes into bite-size chunks. Put in saucepan with onions and add just enough water to cover them. Simmer uncovered until tender, about 15-20 minutes.

Meanwhile, melt remaining 3 T. butter in saucepan. Stir in flour to make a thick paste. Cook for about 30 seconds over medium heat. Slowly add milk, stirring in a bit at a time until blended. Bring to a simmer and simmer for about a minute, until slightly thickened.

Add to potatoes, stir. Serve, topped with bacon bits, chopped green onions, and shredded cheddar cheese.

Potato Cheese Soup

The Basic Potato Soup, on steroids.

2 T. butter
4 oz. ham, chopped
1 c. chopped carrot
8 c. peeled and coarsely chopped potatoes (russets or Yukon Golds)
3 c. chicken broth (or water)
1 c. beer
3/4 c. (3 oz.) grated Gruyere cheese
3/4 c. grated cheddar cheese
1/2 c. milk

(continued on next page)

Melt butter in large saucepan. Add ham, onion and carrot. Sauté 5-10 minutes. Cook, covered, 10 minutes. Add potatoes and broth; cover and simmer 20 minutes or until potatoes are tender.

Pour half the soup into a food processor or blender and process until smooth. (Or use immersion blender.) Return to saucepan. Add beer and cheese and cook until cheese melts. Add milk until desired consistency is reached. Makes 11 cups.

Nacho Spuds

An appetizer or a main dish.

2 large baking potatoes, sliced in 1/2" rounds
2-1/2 T. olive oil
1/2 to 1 pound ground beef
1/2 can black beans, rinsed
2 T. taco seasoning
2 c. shredded sharp cheddar cheese
1 c. cherry tomatoes, quartered
Sour cream, shredded lettuce, taco sauce – for serving

Preheat oven to 450°. Brush potato slices with olive oil; salt and pepper. Arrange in single layer on cookie sheet and bake until golden, about 20 minutes.

Meanwhile, cook burger. Mix in beans, taco seasoning and 2 T. water. Simmer about 10 minutes.

Sprinkle half the cheese on the potatoes. Spoon on the meat mixture. Top with tomatoes and remaining cheese. Place in oven and turn off the heat. Let stand 2-3 minutes until cheese melts. Serve with sour cream, shredded lettuce, taco sauce.

RASPBERRIES

There are a few U-Pick raspberry farms on Old Mission if you don't have your own berry patch. Be sure to stock up when they are fresh in July.

Preparation Libation:

Just about any Peninsula white wine will go great with raspberries. Try ***Black Star Arcturos Chardonnay****.*

Picking and Storing Raspberries

Berries should be ripe, but not over-ripe. They should have turned their full red color and will be easy to pluck off the plant—yet not be so ripe that they crumble. When perfectly ripe, they will almost melt in your mouth when you hold them on your tongue. Rinse if they need it and drain well. (We like to pick soon after a rain so we don't have to wash them.)

They'll keep in the refrigerator for several days, in a ventilated shallow container. Long term, you'll need to freeze them, or make jelly or cordial.

They are easy to freeze—just place berries in quart freezer bags and freeze. Then use for smoothies and in recipes.

Red Raspberry Cordial

This is another colorful Christmas drink—if it lasts that long at your house!

Warm up 3 c. vodka and 2 c. sugar in sauce pan just until sugar dissolves and mixture is clear. Put raspberries in a glass container and cover with vodka mixture. Cover and keep in cool, dark place 3 weeks. Strain and put in glass jars.

Raspberry Jelly

You can make jam out of raspberries, but most kids don't like the seeds in it. So jelly is a better option.

Fill large mixing bowl with berries. Crush until juicy. Strain through a sieve, then strain through cheese cloth. Measure 4 c. of juice.

Prepare 8 oz. jars and get the hot water bath canner boiling. Put berries in a large pot. Add 1 box Sure Jell and 1 t. butter. Bring to full rolling boil.

Add 5-1/2 c. sugar all at once. Bring to full rolling boil and boil 1 minute. Ladle into jars, leaving 1/8" headroom. Seal. Put in hot water bath canner and boil 5-10 minutes.

Raspberry Riesling Jelly

Riesling adds a crisp, Northern Michigan twist to your jelly.

Prep jelly jars. Fill large mixing bowl with berries. Crush. Make a syrup with 3 c. sugar and 1 c. Riesling by boiling for 1 minute. Pour over berries and let soak 3 hours. Drain in wire colander to get 4 c. liquid. Strain with cheese cloth.

Add package of Sure-Jell and 1 t. butter. Bring to a full rolling boil. Quickly add 5-1/2 c. sugar. Bring back to full rolling boil and boil 1 minute.

Put in 8 oz. jelly jars, leaving 1/8" headroom. Boil in hot water bath canner 10 minutes.

Raspberry Daiquiris

1 6-oz. can frozen lemonade or limeade concentrate
1 juice can light rum
1/4 to 1/2 c. powdered sugar
3 c. ice cubes
Lime or lemon wedges
2 c. frozen red raspberries

In a blender, combine lemonade or limeade concentrate, rum, powdered sugar, and raspberries. Add ice cubes a few at a time, through the lid opening, until slushy. Makes 6 servings.

Sparkling Raspberry Lemonade

4 c. water
1 pint (2 c.) raspberries
1-3/4 c. sugar
1 quart lemonade
1 bottle sparkling water
2 c. vodka (optional)

Bring water, raspberries, and sugar to a boil in a large saucepan, stirring occasionally, until sugar dissolves. Reduce heat, and let simmer for 15 minutes. Strain mixture through a strainer, pressing gently. Discard solids. Let syrup cool completely. Combine syrup and lemonade in a large pitcher. Divide among 16 ice-filled glasses. Top each with sparkling water, and vodka if desired. Garnish with fresh raspberries.

Raspberry Sorbet with Whipped Cream

This is a great way to use your frozen raspberries.

1/4 c. water
14 c. plus 1 T. sugar
12 oz./3 c. fresh or frozen raspberries (frozen is better)
1/2 c. whipped cream

Stir together water and 1/4 c. sugar until dissolved. Pulse raspberries in food processor until coarsely chopped. With machine running, pour in sugar water. Pulse until smooth. Transfer to airtight container and freeze until firm – about 1 hour. Whip cream and 1 T. sugar with electric mixer until peaks form. Scoop raspberry sorbet into 4 glasses and top with whipped cream.

Raspberry Pie

3 c. fresh raspberries
1/2 c. sugar
4 t. cornstarch
8 oz. cream cheese, softened (low fat)
1 c. whipped topping
1 c. powdered sugar
1 pie crust – graham cracker or shortbread

Mash 2 c. berries in sauce pan. Add granulated sugar, cornstarch and ¼ c. water. Bring to boil, stirring constantly. Cook, stirring, for 2 minutes. Cool to room temp.

Beat cream cheese, whipped topping and powdered sugar in bowl until smooth. Spread evenly over bottom of pie crust. Arrange remaining berries around the edge. Spoon cooled raspberry sauce over the top. Garnish with fresh berries.

Raspberry Cream Pie

A quick and easy dessert. Thanks to Carol for the recipe!

2 heaping cups fresh raspberries
1 c. whipping cream
1 c. sugar
2 heaping T. flour

Mix sugar and flour then add cream. Put in pie shell. Add berries. Bake at 450° 10-15 minutes, then at 350° for 35-50 minutes, until center is set and a knife inserted comes out clean.

Raspberry Cream Tart

1 tube of refrigerated sugar cookie dough, cut into 1/2 inch thick slices
2 3-oz. packages cream cheese, softened
1/4 c. granulated sugar
1 egg
1 t. finely shredded lemon peel
1 T. lemon juice
1/2 t. vanilla
2 c. fresh red raspberries
2 t. granulated sugar
Powdered sugar

Press cookie dough slices into bottom of a greased pizza pan. Bake in a 350 degree oven 15 minutes or until light brown.

In small mixing bowl, beat cream cheese with electric mixer for 30 seconds. Add ¼ c. sugar, egg, lemon peel, lemon juice and vanilla. Beat until combined. Pour cheese mixture over warm crust and spread evenly.

(continued on next page)

Place the 2 c. raspberries in a single layer on top of cheese mixture. Sprinkle raspberries with 2 t. sugar. Bake for 15-17 minutes more or until cheese mixture is set. Let cool for 30 minutes before serving. Just before serving, sprinkle with powdered sugar. Garnish with additional fresh berries.

Raspberry Snack Bars

2 c. fresh or frozen raspberries
2 T. sugar
2 T. water
1 T. lemon juice
1/2 t. cinnamon
1 c. flour
1 c. quick-cooking rolled oats
2/3 c. packed brown sugar
1/4 t. ground cinnamon
1/8 t. baking soda
1/2 c. butter, melted

For filling:
In a medium saucepan combine berries, sugar, water, lemon juice and 1/2 t. cinnamon. Bring to a boil. Reduce heat. Simmer for about 8 minutes or till slightly thickened, stirring frequently. Remove from heat.

For bars:
In a mixing bowl, stir together flour, oats, brown sugar, 1/4 t. cinnamon and baking soda. Stir in melted butter until thoroughly combined. Set aside 1 c. of the oat mixture for topping. Press remaining oat mixture into an ungreased 9" pan. Bake in a 350° oven for 20-25 minutes.

Carefully spread filling on top of baked crust. Sprinkle with reserved oat mixture and lightly press into filling. Bake in the 350° oven for 20-25 minutes more or till topping is set. Cool in pan, then cut into bars. Makes about 18 bars.

RHUBARB

Once you get a good stand of rhubarb going, it will produce forever (or maybe it just seems that way!)

Preparation Libation:

Sip on some ***Pinot Noir from Brys Estates*** *while chopping up your rhubarb.*

Picking and Storing Rhubarb

Cut stalks when they are a deep pink color, for rhubarb that is good in sweeter recipes. Chop into 1/2 inch slices and use in recipes, make jam, or freeze to use later.

Rhubarb Custard Bars

Thanks to Sue for this tasty dessert.

Crust:
1-1/2 C. flour
1/2 c. sugar
1/2 t. salt
9T chilled butter, cut in small pieces

Combine flour, sugar and salt in a bowl. Cut in butter with pastry blender until mixture resembles coarse meal. Press into 13 x 9 baking dish coated with cooking spray. Bate at 350° for 15 minutes or until brown.

Filling:
1/2 c. flour
1-1/2 c. sugar
1-1/2 c. milk
3 eggs
5 c. fresh or frozen rhubarb, cut in 1/2" slices

Combine sugar and flour in large bowl. Add milk and eggs, stirring with a whisk. Stir in rhubarb. Pour mixture over crust. Bake at 350° for 40 min. or until set. Cool at room temperature.

Topping:
1/2 c. sugar
8 oz. low fat cream cheese
1/2 t. vanilla extract
1 c. frozen fat-free whipped topping, thawed

Beat sugar, cheese, and vanilla in a bowl until smooth. Fold in whipped topping. Spread evenly over baked custard. Cover and chill at least 1 hour.

Rhubarb Custard Pie

1-1/2 c. rhubarb, diced
2 T. flour
3/4 c. cream
1 c. sugar
2 eggs

Preheat oven to 350°. In a large bowl, mix all ingredients except rhubarb. Put rhubarb in unbaked 9" pie shell and pour mixture over the rhubarb. Bake for 45 minutes or until set.

STRAWBERRIES

Don't even bother eating those tasteless grocery store berries in the winter time. Home-grown, fresh-out-of-the garden strawberries cannot be beat!

Preparation Libation:

*Sip on some **Chateau Grand Traverse Late Harvest Riesling** when processing your berries. Plop a few berries in the glass, too, while you're at it.*

Picking and Storing Strawberries

Pick when fully ripe/red, and not mushy. Keep in refrigerator 2-3 days in a ventilated container. Don't rinse until you are ready to use. The best way to save strawberries is to freeze them. They can then be thawed and used in recipes, smoothies, etc.

Freezing Berries

Medium-sized berries work best for freezing. Use quart-sized containers or bags. Cut the tops off the berries and cut in half. Place in container and sprinkle with a couple tablespoons of sugar.

Or you can mash the berries, stir in sugar to taste, and freeze the sauce in plastic containers.

Strawberry Daiquiri

Another "healthy" drink.

1 small can frozen limeade or lemonade
1 small can rum
About 10 oz. frozen strawberries
12-15 ice cubes

Put all in blender and blend until smooth.

Strawberry Riesling Punch

This is a nice punch for an event like a bridal shower.

In bottom of punch bowl, mix 3 c. strawberries (hulled and halved) with 1/4 c. powdered sugar. Let sit a few minutes.

Add:
1 bottle Riesling wine, chilled
1 bottle white sparkling wine, chilled
2 cans of 7-up, chilled
Ice cubes

Serve immediately. Put berries in each glass.

Strawberry Smoothie #1

3/4 c. skim milk
1 small banana
1 small carton vanilla yogurt
1 T. honey
1 c. frozen strawberries

Put in blender and blend until smooth.

Strawberry Smoothie #2

This is a standard breakfast on the 17-Day Diet.

1 c. frozen strawberries (can also use blueberries or raspberries)
1 c. vanilla-flavored Kefir
1 T. agave nectar (or honey)

Put in blender and blend until smooth. If you like it sweeter, add 1 packet of Truvia.

Strawberry Jam

5 c. cleaned and crushed strawberries
7 c. sugar
1 pkg. Sure-Jell
1/2 t. butter

Wash jars, lids, and screw bands in hot, soapy water. Put enough water in canner to cover jars by at least an inch and bring to boil. Prepare fruit and measure out sugar.

Put fruit in large saucepot. Stir Sure-Jell into the fruit and add butter. Bring to a full rolling boil (doesn't stop boiling when you stir it.) Stir sugar in all at once. Return to full rolling boil and boil exactly 1 minute, stirring constantly. Remove from heat.

Immediately ladle into jars, leaving 1/8 inch headroom. Put on lids and bands, wiping any spillover from the jar edges. Place jars into canner. Boil 10 minutes. Remove jars and place on a towel to cool. Can store on shelf out of sunlight for up to a year. Once open, refrigerate and use within 3 weeks.

Strawberry Riesling Jam

This adds a crisp taste to regular jam.

Make a syrup with 3 c. sugar and 1 c. Riesling by mixing and boiling for 1 minute.

Pour over 5-6 c. berries and let soak about 3 hours. Drain and discard most of the liquid. Mash the berries. Cook berries with 1 t. lemon juice, 1 t. butter and 1 pkg. Sure-Jell. Bring to full rolling boil.

Add 4 c. sugar and return to full rolling boil for 1 minute. Ladle in jars, filling to 1/8 inch of the top. Process in hot water bath canner for 10 minutes.

Summer Strawberry Salad

A beautiful, seasonal side dish.

4 c. romaine lettuce, torn
1/2 c. pineapple tidbits, drained
3/4 c. sliced fresh strawberries
1/4 c. mandarin oranges, drained
1/4 c. fresh blueberries
1/4 c. chopped pecans
1/4 c. poppy seed salad dressing

Arrange lettuce on 4 salad plates. Top with the fruits. Sprinkle with pecans. Drizzle with dressing.

Pretzel Jello

Is it a salad? Is it a dessert? Who cares—eat it both ways!

2 c. pretzels, broken
1 c. sugar, plus 3 T.
1 stick butter, melted
1 large box strawberry Jello
2 c. boiling water
28 oz. frozen strawberries
8 oz. cream cheese (at room temperature)
8 oz. Cool Whip

Mix and press pretzels, 3 T. sugar and butter in bottom of 9 x 13 pan. Bake at 375° for 10 minutes.

Mix Jello and boiling water; cool until partially set. Add frozen strawberries. Refrigerate.

Beat cream cheese and 1 c. sugar until smooth. Add Cool Whip. Put cream cheese mixture over pretzel mix. Add set Jello to top of cool whip/cream cheese mix. Refrigerate.

Strawberry Chicken Salad

1 pkg. (5 oz.) salad greens mix
1/2 c. cubed pineapple chunks
1 small red onion, thin sliced
12 oz. cooked chicken breast strips
2 tomatoes, seeded and chopped
1 cucumber, chopped
1 pint fresh strawberries, sliced
3/4 c. crumbled blue cheese
3/4 c. raspberry vinaigrette

Place salad greens in large clear salad bowl. In rows, arrange the onion, pineapple, chicken, tomatoes, cucumber, and strawberries. Sprinkle with blue cheese. Just before serving, drizzle with vinaigrette. Serves 10.

Strawberry Pie

This is very similar to Big Boy's strawberry pie.

3/4 c. sugar
1/2 c. unsweetened cranberry juice
1/4 c. cornstarch
1/4 t. salt
2 qt. fresh strawberries, sliced

Combine in sauce pan 2 c. of the strawberries and all other ingredients. Cook over medium-high heat, gently crushing the berries. Bring to a boil, stirring often. Simmer until thick.

Take off the heat. Stir in remaining berries. Pour into a graham cracker or shortbread pie crust shell. Chill.

Topping:
8 oz. carton whipping cream
1 t. vanilla
1/4 c. sugar

Beat with mixer until soft peaks form. Spread on pie. Garnish with fresh berries.

Strawberry Cake

This is a good summer birthday cake.

Cake:
1 box white cake mix
1 small box strawberry Jello
4 eggs
1/4 t. salt
1 c. crushed strawberries (fresh or frozen)
3/4 c. vegetable oil

(continued on next page)

Icing:
1/2 c. butter, softened
1/2 c. crushed strawberries
Powdered sugar (about half a bag)

Beat cake ingredients for two minutes. Bake in 2 greased 9" layer pans at 350° for 35 minutes. Cool. Beat icing and spread over cooled cake.

Fruit Pizza

This is a 4th of July weekend dessert favorite! Red, white and blue—and fun to eat.

1 tube refrigerated sugar cookie dough
8 oz. pkg. cream cheese, softened
1/2 c. powdered sugar
1 t. lemon juice
1 21-oz. can cherry pie filling
Fresh sliced strawberries, blueberries, and/or raspberries

Let dough stand at room temperature 10 minutes. Press onto ungreased 12" pizza pan. Bake at 350° for 12 minutes until set and lightly browned. Cool. In small bowl, beat cream cheese, sugar and lemon juice. Spread over crust. Top with pie filling. Arrange berries on top. Chill at least 1 hour before serving.

Tropical Berry Pops

2 c. white grape juice or apple juice
1 8-oz. can crushed pineapple
1/2 c. sliced fresh strawberries
1/2 c. other berries—raspberries or blueberries

In a blender, mix juice and undrained crushed pineapple. Divide berries among 12 4-6 oz. popsicle molds. Pour blended mixture over berries. Freeze about 6 hours or until firm.

Dark Chocolate Strawberry Fondue

1/2 lb. semisweet or bittersweet chocolate
3/4. C. cream
1 quart strawberries

Coarsely chop the chocolate and put in a metal bowl. Set aside. In a saucepan, bring the cream to a simmer over medium heat. Pour cream over the chopped chocolate and let stand 5 minutes. Stir with a whisk until smooth. Serve with strawberries.

Easy Chocolate-Covered Berries

Pick out your best large, ripe berries. Leave the stems on. Rinse and dry thoroughly on paper towels.

Melt baker's chocolate in the microwave, per package directions. Can use dark chocolate, white chocolate, or milk chocolate. Dip berries in melted chocolate, then put on waxed paper to cool and harden. These don't keep well, so serve the same day.

Basic Strawberry Shortcake

The plain-old favorite way to eat strawberries.

Cut tops off a quart of berries and mash, using a potato masher. Add sugar to taste and let sit in refrigerator at least an hour.

For the shortcake:
2 c. Bisquick
4 T. sugar
2/3 c. milk

(continued on next page)

Preheat oven to 475°. Mix shortcake dough and drop dough by heaping tablespoons onto ungreased cookie sheet. Bake 10-12 minutes until lightly browned.

Split and top with berries. Serve with either Cool Whip, whipped cream, ice cream, or milk. Some folks like to add milk to the strawberry sauce before serving.

Deluxe Strawberry Shortcake

This could also be made as cupcakes, using the filling as frosting, topped with berries.

Cake:
1 pkg. (18-1/4 oz.) yellow cake mix
1 c. water
1/2 c. sour cream
1/3 c. vegetable oil
3 eggs
1 t. vanilla

Combine in a mixing bowl and beat on low for 30 seconds. Then beat on medium for 2 minutes. Pour into 2 greased and floured 9-in. round baking pans. Bake at 350° for 20-25 minutes or until toothpick inserted near the center comes out clean. Cool for at least 10 minutes before removing from pans.

Filling:
1 pkg. 8 oz. cream cheese, softened
1/3 c. sugar
1 carton Cool Whip, thawed
3 c. chopped fresh strawberries

In small bowl, beat cream cheese and sugar until smooth. Fold in Cool Whip. Place one cake on a serving plate; top with half of the cream cheese mixture and strawberries. Repeat layers. Store in the refrigerator.

TOMATOES

We wait all year for summer tomatoes—no anemic-looking, woody tasting winter tomatoes on our table!

Preparation Libation:

For something fun and different, try ***Chateau Chantal Gewurztraminer*** *with your 'maters.*

Picking and Storing Tomatoes

Let tomatoes stay on the vine until fully red and ripe before picking. If you need to pick sooner, they will ripen on your countertop (upside down) or in a paper bag. If you are going to can the tomatoes, pick when they are still firm and not soft, so their acidity will be higher. Don't refrigerate. Tomatoes will keep up to a week at room temperature. To preserve, they can be frozen or canned.

Freezing Tomatoes

Rinse medium-sized tomatoes. Cut off tops and cut out any bad spots. Place in gallon freezer bags and freeze.

When thawed, you can use them in chili or soup. With chili, blend thawed tomatoes and their liquid in a blender before adding to chili. To use in tomato soup, drain and squeeze out the extra liquid from the thawed tomatoes.

Tomato Juice

We have friends who actually have a tomato juice canning party each year, using this recipe. Of course, the first batch goes right into Bloody Mary's….

Run tomatoes through an electric juicer, enough for a large pot of juice.

Boil juice for 10 minutes. Put 1-1/2 t. canning salt in bottom of clean, sterilized quart canning jars. Pour in the juice. Seal, and boil jars for 45 minutes.

V-8 Tomato Juice

Rinse enough tomatoes to almost fill a large cooking pot. Cut off tops and bad spots. Cut into quarters and place in large cooking pot.

Add to tomatoes:
8 medium carrots, diced
6 medium onions, diced
3 large green peppers, diced
3 large red peppers, diced
3-4 stalks celery, diced
1 small red hot pepper, diced (or 1 T. Tabasco sauce)
4-5 cloves garlic
Handful of fresh parsley
1/2 t. Worcestershire Sauce
2 t. paprika

Cook until veggies are softened. Run mixture through a blender, then through a strainer. Put juice back on the stove and add 1 t. of salt per quart of juice. Boil and keep skimming real thick juice off the top. Put in quart canning jars and seal. Boil in water bath 35 minutes.

Spaghetti Sauce

Thanks to Connie for this recipe. It sure is nice in the winter time to pull down a jar of home-made spaghetti sauce and have a little taste of the summer.

4 cloves garlic (or equivalent chopped garlic from a jar)
3 c. chopped onions
3/4 c. vegetable oil or olive oil
16 c. seeded, chopped tomatoes (Romas are best)
4 – 12 oz. cans tomato paste
4-5 c. water
4 t. sugar
2 T. salt
1 T. pepper
2 T. leaf oregano
4 bay leaves

Cook onion and garlic in oil until tender. Stir in rest of ingredients and simmer 1 hour, uncovered, stirring frequently. Remove bay leaves. (If you don't like chunky marinara sauce, run through a blender, or use immersion blender before putting in jars)

Put in quart canning jars, filling to 1/2 inch of top; seal, and boil in hot water bath for 30 minutes. Can use for any recipe that calls for marinara or pizza sauce.

Gazpacho

The next three recipes are a good use for lots of fresh veggies.

2 lb. ripe tomatoes, coarsely chopped
1 red bell pepper, coarsely chopped
1/2 small red onion, coarsely chopped
1 clove garlic
1 cucumber, coarsely chopped
14 c. olive oil
2 t. red wine vinegar
2 T. chopped fresh flat-leaf parsley
1-1/2 t. salt (sea salt or Kosher)
1/2 t. black pepper

In a blender, working in batches, puree the tomatoes, pepper, onion, garlic, and half of the cucumber. Transfer to a bowl in stir in the oil, vinegar, salt, and pepper. Refrigerate at least an hour, and up to 1 day.

When serving, top with parsley and remaining cucumber. Drizzle with additional olive oil.

Summer Garden Salsa

Cook until onion is tender but not brown:
3 T. olive oil
2-1/2 c. onion, chopped
1 c. sweet red pepper, chopped
1/2 c. jalapeno pepper, chopped

(continued on next page)

Stir in:
2 c. fresh cooked corn
2 c. cucumber, chopped
1 c. parsley, chopped
10 c. tomatoes, chopped
1/4 c. lime juice
1/4 c. honey
1 t. basil
1 t. salt
1 t. chili powder

Bring to boil and simmer 2 minutes. Strain. Yields 8 c.

Gazpacho Salsa

2 Roma tomatoes, seeded and diced
1 yellow bell pepper, diced
1 cucumber, diced
1/2 red onion, diced
1 T. red wine vinegar
1 T. extra-virgin olive oil
Kosher salt and black pepper

In bowl, combine all ingredients. Yields 3 cups.

Tomato Salad

You'd pay an absurd price for this salad at a fancy steak house, but it wouldn't be any better than fresh out of your garden.

Thick-sliced tomatoes, red and yellow, or all one kind
Sea salt or coarse salt
Fresh-ground black pepper
1/2 small red onion, thinly sliced and separated into rings
1 cucumber, halved lengthwise, thinly sliced
1/4 c. loosely packed shredded basil leaves
Snipped fresh chives

(continued on next page)

Arrange tomatoes on serving plates. Sprinkle with salt and pepper. Top with onion, cucumber and basil leaves. Sprinkle with chives. Top with dressing if desired—blue cheese or your favorite vinaigrette. Or you could just sprinkle with Mozzarella. Serve immediately.

Blue Cheese Dressing:
In blender or food processor, combine 1/3 c. milk, 1 t. lemon juice, and 1/2 t. minced garlic. Blend until smooth. Transfer to bowl; stir in 1/4 c. crumbled blue cheese. Serve immediately or store in refrigerator up to 1 week.

Simple Chili

This is my winter go-to meal. Just keep the ingredients on hand and you can come up with dinner in 15 minutes. You could substitute a large can of canned tomatoes, with liquid, for the frozen tomatoes.

1 lb. hamburger
1 onion, chopped
1 packet chili seasoning
1 large can (30 oz.) chili beans
1 gallon-size bag of frozen tomatoes (with their liquid), thawed and run through blender

Brown hamburger with the onion. Stir in chili seasoning packet, chili beans, and tomatoes. Salt and pepper to taste. Simmer.

I went on a diet, swore off drinking and heavy eating,
and in 14 days I lost two weeks.

-Joe E. Lewis

Tomato Gouda Soup

The Gouda cheese makes this nice and smooth-tasting. Try it with smoked Gouda and some chopped pepperoni, too.

Cook together for 5 minutes:
1 small chopped onion (lightly browned in butter.)
2. c. tomatoes (about 1 gallon-size bag, thawed, drained very well and blended in blender—or one large can of canned tomatoes, drained)
1 t. salt
2 T. sugar
1/2 c. pizza sauce or canned spaghetti sauce

Meanwhile:
Melt 2 T. butter and cook with 2 T. flour for a few minutes.
Add 2 c. milk gradually and heat, but don't boil.
Shred 3/4 c. Gouda or smoked Gouda cheese into the pan and heat until cheese is melted.

Add the milk and cheese mixture to the tomato mixture and heat together, but don't boil. Serve with more shredded Gouda and/or croutons for garnish. You can also add chopped bacon bits or pepperoni for the carnivores in the family.

ZUCCHINI AND SQUASH

We don't grow these because we just don't eat them that much. So I combed my church cookbooks to come up with a few recipes that look pretty good.

Picking and Prepping

Given that we really don't eat these in our house, here is my recommendation for handling zucchini and squash:

- *Pick when they look like they are ready*
- *Put zucchini and squash in a cardboard box*
- *Make up a "FREE" sign, and put box at the end of your driveway*
- *With any luck, zucchini will be gone by the next morning.*

Parmesan Zucchini Oven Fries

1-1/2 pounds zucchini, trimmed
1/2 c. flour
2 t. kosher salt, divided
3/4 t. black pepper, divided
3 eggs
1-1/2 c. bread crumbs
1/2 c. grated Parmesan cheese
1 T. chopped dill (optional)

Preheat oven to 425°. Line 2 rimmed baking sheets with parchment paper. Cut zucchini into thick French-fry-size sticks, about 3" long.

Arrange 3 shallow, side bowls or pie plates in a row. In the first bowl, stir together flour, 1 t. salt, and 1/2 t. pepper. In the second bowl, whisk together eggs, 1/2 t. salt and 1/4 t. pepper. In the third bowl, mix bread crumbs, Parmesan, dill and 1/2 t. salt.

Working in batches, first dip zucchini in flour, shaking off excess. Then dip in egg mixture until coated. Then coat in the crumb mixture.

Arrange on pans in a single layer. Bake 15 minutes (on middle and lower oven racks.) Then rotate the pans. Continue to bake until golden and crisp, about 7-12 minutes more.

Try It You'll Like It Zucchini

1 large yellow or white onion, sliced
2 or 3 zucchinis
1 T. butter
3 slices Velveeta cheese

Cook sliced onion in butter, in a large skillet, until soft and slightly browned. Slice zucchini in half-inch slices (do not peel). Place on top of onion, and salt and pepper it. Cover and cook only until squash is tender, about 10 minutes. Place cheese slices over zucchini, cover, and cook over low heat 2-3 minutes to melt the cheese.

Zucchini Casserole

3 or 4 tomatoes, sliced
5 T. brown sugar
Sliced zucchini (slice amount desired)
1 onion, thinly sliced
1/2 t. salt
Velveeta cheese or Cheez Whiz
2-1/2 c. bread crumbs
6 T. butter, melted

In greased 9 x 13" pan, lay the tomato slices and sprinkle with brown sugar. Next, layer the zucchini and onion, alternating to cover tomatoes. Sprinkle with salt. Dot the top with cheese as desired. Mix bread crumbs with butter and put over the top. Bake at 350° for 45 minutes.

Acorn Squash

3 medium acorn squash
1 c. boiling water
2 T. butter
Ground black pepper, to taste

Preheat oven to 400°. Cut each squash in half and scoop out seeds and fibers. Slice a small piece off the bottom of each half so that they will not roll over. Place squash halves, cut side down in shallow casserole dish. Pour boiling water into casserole dish and cover tightly with aluminum foil. Bake 45 minutes or until squash is soft when pierced with a fork. Turn squash cut-side up and fill each half with 1 t. butter. Bake for 5 minutes more, grind pepper over squash and serve.

ADDITIONAL INFORMATION

Abbreviations:

For all recipes, the abbreviations mean the following:

c. = cup
t. = teaspoon
T. = tablespoon

Canning:

If you are new to canning, I'd strongly recommend getting a book explaining the process in more detail. The Ball Blue Book Guide to Home Canning and Freezing is an example of a good one. The instructions that come in the boxes of Sure-Jell are also pretty complete. None of the recipes in this book require pressure canning—only hot water bath canning.

Cooking 101:

The recipes in this book are fairly easy to make. But if you are completely new to cooking and some instructions don't make sense, you may want to seek out a little extra help. Check out the Food Network TV show and web site, the Better Homes and Gardens web site, or the Real Simple web site for basic tips and guidance. Or call someone you know who is a really good cook—they'll be flattered that you asked!

Adding to The Old Mission Cook:

Is your favorite fresh produce recipe missing from this book? If so, email it to me at keith@mileader.com and we'll build a second edition with local favorites.

ABOUT THE AUTHOR

Michelle (Shelley) Keith and her partner Tim Quinn live on a farm on Old Mission, where they have a big garden, a small orchard, and several acres of Riesling and Pinot Gris grapes. They also raise a few animals, including feeder calves, two horses, a flock of chickens, two barn cats, and two Labrador retrievers.

Shelley and Tim have written books on educational leadership, but this is her first book on cooking.

Made in the USA
Charleston, SC
03 May 2012